I0436572

Financial Knowledge for Young Adults Made Easy:

Learn How to Invest, Manage, and Save Money to Create a Safe and Independent Future

By

Kenneth D. Truonggs

TABLE OF CONTENTS

Introduction

I would like to take this opportunity to welcome you to a game-changing journey, one that will lead to your financial independence and prosperity. Understanding the language of money is not only an option for you as a young adult who is navigating the thrilling yet tough waters of independence, job advancement, and personal growth; rather, it is your passport to a future in which you will be financially empowered.

When it comes to demystifying the often complicated environment of financial literacy, "Financial Knowledge for Young Adults Made Easy" is the go-to resource you should consult in a world that feeds on information. In contrast to a boring lecture on budgeting or a normal crash course in economics, this is not one of those things. However, you should think of it as your roadmap, which will lead you through the twists and turns of managing your finances, making decisions based on accurate information, and establishing a foundation for long-term financial well-being.

Financial Knowledge for Young Adults Made Easy

We are here to help you overcome the obstacles that stand in the way of your financial awareness, whether it be clever investing methods that speak to your goals or budgeting techniques that won't make your life more challenging. There will be no usage of jargon or difficult formulas; rather, there will be plain insights that are intended to resonate with the vibrant and ambitious attitude of today's young adults.

Therefore, whether you are imagining a future in which you are financially independent, planning your business venture, or dreaming of your first apartment, "Financial Knowledge for Young Adults Made Easy" should be your friend. At this point, it is time to transform the intimidating idea of financial literacy into a reality that empowers individuals. You are about to embark on a trip that will lead to a greater and more wealthy future, so get ready to uncover the secrets, take control of your financial destiny, and get things started!

Chapter 1

Knowledge of Finances

Literacy in financial matters is an essential component of both personal empowerment and appropriate management of one's financial resources. Specifically, it involves the information and abilities required to make decisions with money that are both educated and effective. In its most basic form, financial literacy refers to the ability to earn, save, invest, and prudently manage money to accomplish one's personal financial goals and successfully traverse the financial hurdles that life could present.

The Cornerstone of Responsible Financial Management:

1. The first step toward achieving financial literacy is gaining an awareness of how to start earning money. The exploration of numerous professional routes, the development of skills and certifications, and the negotiation of fair compensation are all included in this concept.

When it comes to the job market, it is important to acknowledge the value of your time, effort, and experience.

2. Budgeting: At its foundation, financial literacy is about developing and keeping to a budget. A budget is a plan that describes how much money you earn, spend, and save. It helps you organize resources to satisfy your needs, prioritize expenses, and minimize overspending.

3. Saving: Saving money is a crucial part of financial literacy. It entails saving aside a portion of your salary for future needs or emergencies. Understanding the value of saving helps develop a financial safety net and provides a sense of financial security.

4. Investing: Financial literacy extends to the concept of investing, which is using money to earn additional money over time. Investing can take different forms, such as stocks, bonds, real estate, or retirement savings. Knowing the basics of investment possibilities and dangers is key to generating long-term wealth.

5. Understanding Debt: Financial literacy includes knowing how to handle and appropriately use debt. This entails comprehending several sorts of debt, such as credit cards, loans, and mortgages.

It's crucial to borrow prudently, avoid excessive debt, and have a strategy for payback.

Key Components of Financial Literacy

1. Revenue: Financial literacy begins with recognizing your revenue sources, whether it's a paycheck, freelance work, or business income. Knowing how to negotiate salary, pursue career progress, and diversify income streams leads to financial well-being.

2. Budgeting and Spending: Creating a budget entails identifying your income and categorizing expenses. Financial literacy highlights the significance of managing expenditure, distinguishing between requirements and wants, and making informed choices to align spending with priorities.

3. Saving and Emergency Funds: Financial literacy supports the practice of saving money frequently. This involves establishing an emergency fund to handle unforeseen expenses like medical bills or car repairs. Saving for short-term and long-term goals improves financial stability.

4. Banking and Financial Institutions: Understanding how banks and financial institutions operate is part of financial literacy. This includes learning how to open and manage a bank account, understanding interest rates, and being aware of expenses associated with financial services.

5. Credit and Debt Management: Financial literacy comprises understanding credit ratings, how credit works, and the repercussions of carrying debt. Knowing how to manage credit responsibly and make informed borrowing decisions is vital for preserving financial health.

6. Investing Basics: Learning the basics of investing is a critical component of financial literacy. This includes understanding the risk-return trade-off, diversification, and the power of compound interest. Knowing how to identify proper investment options corresponds with long-term financial goals.

7. Retirement Planning: Financial literacy extends to planning for retirement. This entails understanding retirement accounts, employer-sponsored plans, and the need for continuous contributions over time. Knowing how to navigate retirement alternatives helps secure financial security in later years.

8. Insurance: Understanding the importance of insurance in financial planning is part of financial literacy.
This comprises health insurance, life insurance, and property insurance. Knowing how to assess insurance needs and choose adequate coverage is vital.
9. Taxes: Financial literacy includes a basic understanding of taxes. This requires learning how to submit income tax forms, comprehending tax deductions and credits, and budgeting for tax responsibilities.

Importance of Financial Literacy

1. Empowerment: Financial literacy helps individuals to take control of their financial lives. When people understand their financial options and make educated decisions, they are better positioned to achieve their goals and adapt to difficulties.
2. Goal Achievement: Financial literacy helps individuals define and achieve financial goals. Whether it's buying a home, paying for education, or saving for retirement, having financial knowledge enables people to make realistic goals and strive towards their aspirations.
3. Economic Stability: A financially knowledgeable population adds to overall economic stability.

When individuals handle money well, they are less likely to encounter financial crises that could have broader economic effects.

4. Debt Prevention and Management: Financial knowledge plays a critical role in preventing excessive debt and managing existing obligations appropriately. Individuals who understand the ramifications of borrowing are more likely to make informed judgments regarding when and how to use credit.

5. Wealth Building: Building money is a long-term process, and financial literacy is the foundation for making wise investment decisions. Knowing how to invest, diversify portfolios, and take advantage of compounding returns helps individuals develop wealth over time.

6. Decision-Making Skills: Financial literacy promotes decision-making abilities connected to money. Whether it's picking between job offers, deciding on a large purchase, or navigating investment alternatives, individuals with financial understanding may make decisions aligned with their values and priorities.

7. Preparedness for Life Transitions: Life is full of transitions, and financial literacy helps individuals plan for changes such as marriage, parenthood, homeownership, or retirement. Understanding the financial repercussions of life events helps smoother transitions.

8. Reducing Stress: Financial literacy minimizes financial stress. Knowing how to handle money, prepare for the future, and negotiate financial issues minimizes anxiety connected to financial uncertainty.

Practical Tips for Improving Financial Literacy

1. Continuous Learning: Stay curious and consistently educate yourself about personal finance. Read books, and articles, and attend workshops to increase your financial knowledge.

2. Seek Professional Advice: Consult with financial counselors or experts for specialized guidance. Professionals can provide insights suited to your financial condition and aspirations.

3. Use Technology: Leverage technological tools and apps for budgeting, investing, and tracking costs.

Many apps ease money management and provide insights into your spending habits.

4. Set Financial Goals: Clearly outline short-term and long-term financial goals. Setting specific, measurable, attainable, relevant, and time-bound (SMART) goals guides your financial journey.

5. Practice Budgeting: Develop the habit of budgeting frequently. Track your income and expenses, and alter your budget as needed to line up with your financial goals.

6. Diversify Investments: If you're investing, recognize the value of diversity. Spread your investments across several asset classes to lessen risk.

7. Stay Informed about Changes: Keep yourself informed about changes in tax laws, banking regulations, and economic trends. This insight enables you to change your financial tactics properly.

8. Share Knowledge: Share financial knowledge with friends and family. Discussing financial topics publicly helps establish a culture of financial literacy within your community.

9. Build a Support System: Surround yourself with a supportive network of others who have an interest in financial literacy.
Exchange ideas, learn from each other's experiences, and motivate one another to attain financial goals.
10. Learn from Mistakes: - Accept that financial mistakes happen, and use them as opportunities to learn. Reflect on your experiences, find areas for growth, and adapt your financial approach accordingly.

Financial literacy is a lifetime journey that entails acquiring knowledge, developing skills, and making informed money decisions. By knowing the principles of earning, saving, investing, and managing money intelligently, individuals may develop a strong foundation for financial well-being and achieve their life goals. Continuous study, practical application of financial ideas, and obtaining professional assistance contribute to a holistic approach to financial literacy

How early financial decisions impact future financial well-being

Early financial decisions play a key influence in defining future financial well-being. The choices individuals make during their early years can have enduring implications on their financial security, opportunities, and overall quality of life. Here are significant ways in which early financial decisions affect future financial well-being:

1. Establishing Financial Habits:

• Early Influence: The financial habits acquired in adolescence frequently set the pattern for adulthood. Learning to budget, save, and make appropriate spending decisions at an early age provides a foundation for financial discipline.

• Impact on the Future: Individuals who develop healthy financial habits early are more likely to continue these actions throughout their lifetimes. Consistent saving, thoughtful spending, and appropriate credit utilization become ingrained habits that lead to long-term financial well-being.

2. Building a Credit History:
• Early Influence: Establishing a credit history begins with the first financial transactions, such as opening a bank Account or applying for a credit card. Responsible usage of credit in early adulthood adds to a positive credit history.
• Impact on the Future: A healthy credit history is vital for future financial undertakings. It affects the ability to acquire favorable interest rates on loans, access housing, and even impact employability in some fields. Early errors, such as late payments, can have long-lasting implications.
3. Educational Investment:
• Early Influence: Decisions involving education, especially choices about college and student loans, are crucial early financial considerations. Investing in education can open doors to higher-paying opportunities.
• Impact on the Future: The level of education gained frequently correlates with earning potential. However, the financial load of student loans might influence long-term financial well-being. A thoughtful analysis of the return on investment in education is vital.

4. Savings and Investing:

• Early Influence: Initiating savings and investment behaviors early in life affords the advantage of time and compounding. Individuals who start saving for goals like housing or retirement in their early years benefit from the increase of their investments over time.

• Impact on the Future: The force of compounding means that even small amounts saved early can increase dramatically. Early investors can accumulate greater wealth than those who wait for their saving and investing efforts.

5. Career Choices:

• Early Influence: Career decisions made in the early stages of adulthood can considerably affect income levels and overall financial well-being. Factors such as education, skills development, and industry choice play an impact.

• Impact on the Future: Choosing a vocation that corresponds with personal interests, abilities, and market demand can lead to increased income potential and job satisfaction. Conversely, continually switching occupations without a clear goal can impair financial stability.

6. Debt Management:
• Early Influence: Early decisions regarding borrowing and managing debt, such as credit card use and school loans, define an individual's relationship with debt. Accumulating excessive debt early on can become a hardship in later years.
• Impact on the Future: Managing debt wisely is vital for future financial health. Individuals who accrue large debt without a clear repayment strategy may experience difficulty in fulfilling major life goals, such as property or retirement.
7. Lifestyle Choices:
• Early Influence: Lifestyle choices, including housing, transportation, and spending patterns, are influenced by early financial decisions. Overcommitting to a luxury lifestyle or making reckless spending choices might harm financial well-being.
• Impact on the Future: A sustainable lifestyle that matches with one's financial capacity leads to long-term financial well-being. Early decisions concerning housing and spending patterns can affect the potential to save and invest for the future.

8. Emergency Preparedness:

• Early Influence: Building an emergency fund early in one's financial path indicates a commitment to financial preparedness. Understanding the necessity of having a financial buffer for unforeseen expenses is a great lesson.

• Impact on the Future: An emergency fund provides a safety net during unanticipated financial hardships, preventing individuals from succumbing to high-interest loans or derailing long-term financial objectives. Early attention to emergency preparedness develops financial resiliency.

9. Retirement Planning:

• Early Influence: Decisions about retirement money and planning are generally postponed, yet early awareness and action can dramatically affect the retirement lifestyle. Starting to save for retirement in the early working years optimizes the benefits of compounding.

• Impact on the Future: Individuals who prioritize retirement planning early in their careers are more likely to build considerable retirement funds. Delaying retirement contributions can result in the need to catch up later in life, which may be hard.

10. Financial Education and Literacy:
• Early Influence: Exposure to financial education and literacy in the formative years gives individuals the information and abilities to make informed decisions. Learning about budgeting, investing, and financial planning lays the basis for a lifetime of financial competence.
• Impact on the Future: A lack of financial literacy can lead to unwise judgments and missed opportunities. Conversely, persons with a high financial education are more suited to negotiate complex financial landscapes and adapt to changing circumstances.
Early financial decisions form the building blocks of future financial well-being. They shape financial habits, affect possibilities, and define the trajectory of one's financial journey. While it's never too late to make beneficial changes, the impact of early actions highlights the significance of growing financial literacy, making educated choices, and prioritizing long-term financial goals from the outset. As individuals manage the complexity of personal finance, the lessons learned in their early years serve as a guiding force for a financially secure and rewarding future.

Chapter 2.

Understanding Money Mindset

Money is a topic that touches practically every area of our lives, from the roof over our heads to the food on our tables. Yet, it's not just about dollars and cents; it's about our perspective, the prism through which we view and interact with money. Enter the area of "money mindset," a sophisticated interaction of beliefs, attitudes, and actions that impact our financial judgments. We'll go into the topic of money mindset, studying its roots, influence, and practical techniques to create a healthy and empowered relationship with money.

What is Money Mindset?

At its simplest, a money mindset is the mental framework we hold regarding money — a set of beliefs and attitudes that drive our financial activities. It's the secret power directing our financial decisions, from budgeting and saving to investing and spending. Think of it as the software running in the background, determining our responses to financial obstacles and opportunities.

The Roots of Money Mindset: Nature vs. Nurture

Our connection with money isn't born suddenly; it evolves, molded by a multiplicity of circumstances. Two key aspects contribute to the creation of our money mindset: nature and nurture.

1. Nature:

• Some components of our money perspective may be built into our personalities. Are you a natural saver, constantly thinking about the future, or are you more inclined to live in the present, enjoying the results of your labor immediately? These preferences can be impacted by innate personality factors.

2. Nurture:

• The environment in which we grow up profoundly influences our money perspective. Our family's approach to money, societal influences, and early experiences with financial success or challenges all play a part. Did you watch your parents scrupulously planning or spending on occasional luxuries? These early observations form the foundation for your money thinking.

Common Money Mindsets

Money attitudes come in all forms and sizes, each influencing our financial decisions in unique ways.

Let's review some prevalent money mindsets and their characteristics:

1. Scarcity Mindset:

• Belief System: The belief that resources, especially money, are scarce and hard to come by.

• Impact: This leads to anxiety about not having enough, hoarding money, and unwillingness to take financial risks.

2. Abundance Mindset:

• Conviction System: The conviction that there is enough for everyone, and additional prospects for prosperity exist.

• Impact: Encourages charity, a willingness to contribute, and a favorable attitude on financial prospects.

3. Fear of Money:

• Belief System: Associating money with negative emotions, such as worry, anxiety, or guilt.

• Impact: This may lead to avoidance of financial concerns, lack of budgeting, and trouble generating wealth.

4. Money as a Measure of Success:

• Belief System: Equating personal achievement and worth with the quantity of money one obtains.

• Impact: Driven by external affirmation, may lead to a relentless quest for wealth at the expense of personal well-being.

5. Minimalist Mindset:

• Belief System: Embracing simplicity and prioritizing experiences above material goods.

• Impact: Focus on conscious spending, saving for meaningful goals, and less dependency on consumption.

6. Consumerist Mindset:

• Belief System: Linking happiness and fulfillment to the acquisition of material items.

• Impact: Prone to impulse spending, accumulating debt, and a continual pursuit of the latest trends.

7. Financial Independence Mindset:

• Belief System: Prioritizing financial independence and freedom to make life choices.

• Impact: Emphasizes strategic saving, investment, and long-term planning for financial security.

The Impact of Money Mindset on Behavior

Your money attitude isn't simply a theoretical concept; it manifests in your day-to-day financial activities.

Let's study how different money perspectives might shape behaviors:

1. Spending Habits:
• Scarcity Mindset: Tendency to hoard money, dread of spending.
• Abundance Mindset: Comfort with spending on experiences, investments, and self-improvement.

2. Saving Patterns:
• Fear of Money: Reluctance to save due to bad connotations with money.
• Financial Independence Mindset: Diligent saving for financial security and independence.

3. Approach to Debt:
• Consumerist Mindset: Prone to accumulating debt for the sake of purchasing stuff.
• Minimalist Mindset: Intentional and conscientious attitude to debt, prioritizing needs above wants.

4. Attitude toward Investments:
• Scarcity Mindset: Fearful of investment risks, reluctant to pursue investment prospects.
• Abundance Mindset: Willingness to take prudent risks, and investigate varied investment possibilities.

5. Career Choices:

• Money as a Measure of Success: Pursuit of high-paying employment for external recognition.

• Minimalist Mindset: Choosing occupations aligned with personal beliefs, even if less lucrative.

6. Response to Financial Setbacks:

• Scarcity Mindset: Panic and terror in the face of financial misfortunes.

• Abundance Mindset: Resilience and optimism, viewing setbacks as transitory difficulties.

Cultivating a Positive Money Mindset: Practical Strategies:

Understanding your money perspective is the first step toward establishing a healthy and powerful relationship with money. Here are real techniques to modify and enhance your money mindset:

1. Self-Reflection:

• Ask Yourself: What are your first memories relating to money? How do you feel about money, and what messages did you get about it growing up?

2. Identify Limiting Beliefs:

• Challenge Assumptions: Identify any beliefs that limit your financial potential. Are these ideas founded on facts or inherited narratives?

3. Set Financial Goals:

• Define Objectives: Set clear and achievable financial goals. Align your goals with your beliefs, ensuring they reflect what matters to you.

4. Monitor Your Self-Talk:

• Positive Affirmations: Pay attention to your mental discourse about money. Replace negative self-talk with positive affirmations to transform your mentality.

5. Educate Yourself:

• Continuous Learning: Invest time in financial education. Understanding financial principles helps you to make informed judgments.

6. Surround Yourself Positively:

• Choose Influences Wisely: Surround yourself with favorable influences. Engage with individuals who inspire and provide helpful thoughts about money.

7. Practice Gratitude:

• Focus on Abundance: Cultivate a mindset of thankfulness. Acknowledge and appreciate the richness in your life beyond monetary factors.

8. Budget Mindfully:

• Align Spending with Values: Create a budget that reflects your values. Prioritize spending on experiences and goods that bring genuine joy and fulfillment.

9. Embrace Financial Independence:

• Shift attention: Shift your attention from external affirmation to internal fulfillment and financial independence. Define success on your terms.

10. Seek Professional Guidance: - Financial Advisor: Consult with a financial advisor to gain personalized insights. A specialist can provide assistance targeted to your financial position.

11. Embrace missteps as Learning Opportunities: - Learn from Setbacks: View financial missteps as opportunities for progress. Reflect on what you can learn and change your approach accordingly.

12. Visualize Success: - Create a Vision Board: Visualize your financial goals by constructing a vision board.

Include visuals and statements that depict your intended financial future.

13. Celebrate Progress: - Acknowledge Achievements: Celebrate your financial achievements, no matter how modest. Acknowledging progress strengthens positive behaviors.

14. Practice Mindfulness: - Stay Present: Practice mindfulness to stay present and avoid getting overwhelmed by future financial problems. Focus on your present financial decisions.

15. Cultivate Generosity: - Practice Giving: Cultivate an affluence attitude by practicing generosity. This doesn't always mean monetary donations — it might also involve giving time or providing information.

In the enormous geography of personal finance, the topography is as much mental as it is monetary. Your money mindset, created by nature and developed by experiences, is a powerful force steering your financial journey. Understanding, reflecting upon, and actively modifying your money mindset helps you to make decisions that correspond with your beliefs and move you toward financial well-being.

As you embark on this road, remember that it's not about obtaining perfection but about development. Small, focused measures can lead to dramatic shifts in your relationship with money. Embrace the opportunity to create a positive money attitude, and watch as it becomes a compass guiding you toward a future of financial empowerment, fulfillment, and wealth.

Risk Management Mindset

A risk management mindset is a strategic approach to decision-making that involves systematically detecting, assessing, and minimizing risks in various facets of life or business. It's about realizing that uncertainties and potential challenges are inherent in any effort and taking proactive steps to analyze, minimize, and navigate those risks successfully. Whether employed in personal, professional, or financial situations, a risk management mindset comprises an organized and intelligent approach to tackling uncertainty.

Key Elements of a Risk Management Mindset

1. Risk Awareness:

• Identification: A risk management mentality begins with the capacity to detect potential risks. This entails evaluating uncertainties that could affect goals, projects, or activities.

• Understanding Variability: Acknowledge that outcomes are susceptible to variability, and not all events are within your control. Understanding the range of probable outcomes is vital.

2. Risk Assessment:

• Quantification: Evaluate the potential impact and likelihood of identified hazards. This process involves assigning values or probability to distinct possibilities to prioritize and focus efforts.

• Prioritization: Not all risks are of equal relevance. A risk management approach entails prioritizing risks based on their potential impact and likelihood, ensuring that resources are spent appropriately.

3. Risk Mitigation:

• Proactive preparation: Rather than waiting for hazards to occur, a risk management attitude incorporates proactive preparation.

This may include making contingency plans, implementing preventive measures, or diversifying strategies.

• Adaptability: Recognize that the risk landscape can change, and be prepared to alter your strategies accordingly. This may require changing plans, reallocating resources, or installing new risk mitigation measures.

4. Continuous Monitoring:

• Vigilance: A risk management attitude is not a one-time action; it's a continual effort. Continuous monitoring allows for the identification of new risks and the assessment of changes in existing ones.

• Feedback Loops: Establish feedback loops that permit regular assessments of risk management techniques. Learn from experiences, both successes and failures, to refine and improve risk management approaches.

5. Decision-Making under Uncertainty:

• Informed Decision-Making: Embrace the truth that decision-making involves ambiguity. A risk management attitude emphasizes making educated decisions based on the best available information while acknowledging and accounting for uncertainty.

• Balancing Risks and Rewards: Recognize that risk and reward are interconnected. A risk management mindset entails striking the ideal balance between taking risks to achieve goals and developing techniques to avoid any negative effects.

6. Crisis Preparedness:

• Scenario Planning: Consider worst-case situations and prepare plans for crisis management. Being prepared for extreme occurrences ensures a more resilient response in times of unexpected obstacles.

• Communication Strategies: In the face of a crisis, effective communication is crucial. A risk management attitude entails having clear communication plans in place to address stakeholders and manage expectations.

7. Cultural Integration:

• Cultural Values: Foster a risk-aware culture inside organizations or personal spheres. Encourage open communication regarding hazards, and build an environment where individuals feel comfortable reporting concerns.

• Learning from Mistakes: View mistakes not as failures but as chances to learn and develop.

A risk management mindset involves developing a culture of constant development and flexibility.

8. Ethical Considerations:

• Integrity: Incorporate ethical issues into risk management. Ensure that risk reduction measures align with ethical beliefs and comply with legal and regulatory norms.

• Transparency: Maintain transparency in risk communication. Open and honest communication promotes trust among stakeholders and helps manage expectations.

Application of a Risk Management Mindset in Different Contexts

1. Financial Risk Management:

• Diversification: Spread assets across several asset classes to lessen the impact of market volatility.

• Insurance Planning: Purchase insurance to safeguard against financial losses due to unanticipated events such as accidents, health concerns, or natural disasters.

2. Project Management:

• Risk Register: Maintain a complete risk register that identifies, assesses, and monitors project risks throughout its lifecycle.

• Contingency Planning: Develop contingency plans to manage anticipated project disruptions, ensuring that the team is prepared to tackle unexpected obstacles.

3. Personal Finance:

• Emergency Fund: Maintain an emergency fund to cover unforeseen expenses, giving a financial safety net.

• Debt Management: Approach borrowing with a thorough grasp of the risks involved and establish solutions for responsible debt management.

4. Entrepreneurship:

• Market Research: Conduct rigorous market research to discover potential risks and possibilities before beginning a new firm.

• Business Continuity Planning: Develop business continuity plans to guarantee the organization can navigate unanticipated disruptions.

5. Health and Safety:

• Preventative steps: Implement preventative steps to limit the risk of accidents or health difficulties in many settings, from workplaces to residences.

• Compliance: Adhere to safety norms and standards to minimize the risk of legal and regulatory penalties.

Challenges in Cultivating a Risk Management Mindset

While a risk management attitude is vital, it's not without obstacles. Overcoming these challenges is crucial to creating a proactive approach to risk:

1. Overcoming Complacency:

• Challenge: In moments of stability, there may be a propensity to become complacent and overlook potential threats.

• Strategy: Foster a culture of continual risk awareness and emphasize the significance of preparedness even during seemingly stable times.

2. Balancing Risk Aversion:

• Challenge: Excessive risk aversion might limit innovation and progress.

• Strategy: Encourage calculated risk-taking and build a framework that distinguishes between acceptable and unacceptable risks.

3. Addressing Cognitive Biases:

• Challenge: Cognitive biases, such as overconfidence or anchoring, might impair objective risk evaluations.

• Strategy: Implement processes that integrate different viewpoints, leverage data-driven decision-making, and question assumptions to counter cognitive biases.

4. Resource Allocation:

• Challenge: Limited resources may offer obstacles in executing comprehensive risk management techniques.

• Strategy: Prioritize risks based on their potential impact, deploy resources effectively, and explore cost-effective risk mitigation solutions.

5. Resistance to Change:

• Challenge: Resistance to change might hamper the adoption of new risk management measures.

• Strategy: Communicate the benefits of a risk management attitude, provide training and education, and involve key stakeholders in the decision-making process.

A risk management attitude is not about avoiding risks totally but about navigating them wisely. It entails a holistic and proactive approach to uncertainty, integrating risk concerns into decision-making processes, and developing a culture of adaptation and resilience. Whether in personal finance, business, or daily life, having a risk management attitude empowers individuals and

Organizations to meet problems head-on and emerge stronger from unforeseen circumstances. It's a mindset that embraces uncertainty as a vital part of the journey and transforms problems into opportunities for growth and improvement.

Chapter 3.

Understanding the Basics of an Emergency Fund

In the unpredictable journey of life, unexpected events and financial surprises are inevitable. An emergency fund works as a solid safety net, providing a buffer to mitigate the impact of unforeseen expenses. We'll uncover the basics of an emergency fund, covering what it is, why it's necessary, how to develop and maintain it, and its function in your overall financial well-being.

What is an Emergency Fund?

An emergency fund is a specific pool of money set up to handle unforeseen bills or financial emergencies. It serves as a financial safety net, delivering peace of mind and financial security when facing unexpected hardships. Unlike savings allocated for specific aims, an emergency fund is a multipurpose resource meant to cover a range of urgent and unanticipated emergencies.

Why is an Emergency Fund Important?

1. Financial Security: An emergency fund provides a layer of financial stability, ensuring that you have the resources to address unforeseen needs without resorting to high-interest debt or derailing your long-term financial goals.

2. Peace of Mind: Knowing that you have a financial safety net in place brings a piece of mind. It allows you to navigate life's uncertainties with confidence, lowering stress and worries connected with unforeseen financial issues.

3. Avoiding Debt Traps: Without an emergency fund, consumers may be compelled to rely on credit cards or loans to cover sudden bills. This can lead to the accumulation of high-interest debt, creating a cycle that is tough to stop.

4. Flexibility in Decision-Making: Having an emergency fund offers you the ability to make wise financial decisions, especially in unforeseen events. Whether it's a medical emergency, car repair, or sudden job loss, you may address the crisis without jeopardizing your financial stability.

5. Smoothing Income Fluctuations: For those with unpredictable income or freelancers, an emergency fund functions as a buffer during lean months. It helps level your revenue fluctuations, ensuring you can cover important expenses when earnings are variable.

6. Opportunity to Invest Confidently: With an emergency fund in place, you can approach investments with greater confidence. Knowing that you have a financial safety net allows you to invest for the long term without the risk of needing to liquidate assets prematurely.

How Much Should You Save for an Emergency?

Determining the suitable amount for your emergency fund depends on several aspects, including your living expenses, income stability, and unique circumstances. Here are some tips to help you establish the correct size for your emergency fund:

1. Covering Essential Expenses: Aim to save at least three to six months' worth of essential living expenditures. This should cover bills such as rent or mortgage, utilities, groceries, insurance fees, and minimum debt payments.

2. Adjust for Individual Factors: Consider individual issues that may affect the size of your emergency fund.

If you have dependents, a changeable income, or work in an industry with increased employment instability, you may choose a larger fund to allow for future issues.

3. Health Care Considerations: Individuals with health issues or those with greater health care bills may choose to have a larger emergency fund. This guarantees coverage for unanticipated medical bills that can emerge.

4. Job Security: Assess the stability of your work or income source. If your employment is secure and your income is steady, you might lean toward the lower end of the three to six months range. For people in more volatile industries, a greater emergency fund may be beneficial.

5. Evaluate Lifestyle Factors: Lifestyle choices and spending habits play a part in deciding the size of your emergency fund. If you have a minimalist lifestyle and low fixed expenses, you may find that a smaller emergency fund still provides appropriate coverage.

Where to Keep Your Emergency Fund
While accessibility is necessary for an emergency fund, it's also important to ensure that the money is not too quickly accessible, preventing reckless spending. Consider these options for keeping your emergency fund:

1. Savings Account: A standard savings account is a common alternative for an emergency fund. It gives liquidity, ensuring that you may access the funds immediately. Look for accounts with competitive interest rates to help your money grow over time.

2. Money Market Account: Money market accounts combine the convenience of a savings account with somewhat higher interest rates. They generally come with check-writing capabilities, giving flexibility while retaining liquidity.

3. Certificate of Deposit (CD): Certificates of Deposit offer higher interest rates than normal savings accounts, but they come with a trade-off. Your money is locked in for a specified term, and removing it before maturity may entail penalties. Consider laddering CDs to retain accessibility.

4. High-Yield Savings Account: Online banks often provide high-yield savings accounts with competitive interest rates. While they provide liquidity, ensure that the bank is trustworthy and that your funds are FDIC-insured.

5. Cash Reserves in a Safe Location: For further security, consider storing a portion of your emergency money in cash, stored in a secure area.

This can be helpful in case of situations where electronic transactions are momentarily unavailable.

Building Your Emergency Fund: A Step-by-Step Guide

1. Set Clear Goals: Define your financial goals for the emergency fund. This could include saving a specified financial amount or reaching a certain number of months' worth of living costs.

2. Calculate Living Expenses: Determine your necessary living expenditures, including rent or mortgage, utilities, groceries, insurance, and debt payments. This establishes the benchmark for your emergency fund target.

3. Start Small: If saving a considerable sum feels overwhelming, start small. Set attainable monthly savings targets, gradually increasing them as your financial condition improves.

4. Budget Effectively: Create a realistic budget that allows you to allocate a portion of your income to your emergency fund. Identify areas where you can minimize wasteful costs and redirect those dollars to savings.

5. Automate Savings: Set up automatic transfers from your primary account to your emergency fund.

Automation maintains consistency and eliminates the temptation to spend the money intended for emergencies

6. Use Windfalls Wisely: Apply unexpected windfalls, such as tax returns or work bonuses, to your emergency fund. This increases the savings process without compromising your usual budget.

7. Windfall Rule: Consider adopting the "50-30-20" approach, where 50% of unexpected or additional money goes toward needs, 30% toward wants, and 20% directly to savings, including your emergency fund.

8. Side Hustles & Additional Income: Explore side hustles or alternative income streams to bolster your emergency fund. This could involve freelancing work, selling stuff you no longer need, or taking up part-time tasks.

9. Review and Adjust: Periodically assess your budget and emergency fund progress. Adjust your savings objectives as your financial condition evolves, and celebrate milestones along the way.

Maintaining Your Emergency Fund: Best Practices

1. Regularly Reassess Living Expenses: Life conditions change, and so do living expenses.

Regularly review your critical expenses to ensure that your emergency fund is matched with your current financial demands.

2. Replenish after Withdrawals: If you draw into your emergency savings for a valid expense, prioritize rebuilding the fund as quickly as feasible. This ensures that you're always prepared for the next unforeseen incident.

3. Adjust Savings Goals: As your income, spending, or financial goals change, be flexible with your savings goals. Adjust them to fit your current situation and priorities.

4. Keep Track of Windfalls: Windfalls, such as tax returns or work bonuses, provide an ideal opportunity to increase your emergency fund. Ensure that a percentage of unexpected income is continuously dedicated to savings.

5. Review and Optimize: Periodically assess the location of your emergency fund and research solutions that offer competitive interest rates. Optimizing the fund's placement can add to its growth over time.

6. Emergency Fund as a Priority: Treat your emergency savings as a non-negotiable expense.

Prioritize contributions to your fund before devoting funds to discretionary spending or non-essential goods.

7. Communicate with Family: If you share finances with a spouse or family members, convey the necessity of the emergency fund. Ensure that everyone is on the same page on its goal and how contributions will be made.

Emergency Fund and Debt: Balancing Act

While having an emergency fund is critical, it's essential to achieve a balance if you're simultaneously managing debt. Here's how to negotiate this balancing act:

1. Prioritize High-Interest Debt: If you have high-interest debt, such as credit card charges, prioritize paying it down while still making modest contributions to your emergency fund. Once high-interest debt is under control, work on growing the emergency fund more aggressively.

2. Establish a Contingency Plan: If confronting a financial emergency with little savings, having a contingency plan is crucial. This could involve discussing payment plans with creditors or seeking assistance programs while concurrently working to create your emergency fund.

3. Gradual Debt and Savings Allocation: Strive for a balanced approach.

Allocate a percentage of your resources to both debt repayment and emergency fund savings. This assures progress on both fronts without neglecting one over the other.

4. Seek Professional Advice: If managing debt and saving simultaneously feels overwhelming, try receiving guidance from a financial counselor. They can help design a personalized strategy that corresponds with your individual financial condition and aspirations.

Emergency Fund and Investing: When and How?

Once your emergency fund is formed, you may think about the possibility of investing the extra funds. Here are factors on when and how to switch from a traditional savings approach to investing:

1. Fully Funded Emergency Fund: Ensure that your emergency fund is fully funded, covering three to six months' worth of basic living needs, before contemplating investment possibilities.

2. Assess Risk Tolerance: Evaluate your risk tolerance and investment knowledge. Understand that investing necessarily entails risk, and there are no assurances of returns.

3. Diversify Investments: If transitioning to investments, choose a diverse approach. Explore low-risk options, such as index funds or bonds, to balance prospective rewards with risk avoidance.

4. Maintain Liquidity: Keep a portion of your emergency money in liquid, easily accessible assets. This ensures that you have immediate access to funds in case of urgent demands.

5. Consult a Financial Advisor: Before getting into investments, contact a financial counselor. They can provide individualized advice based on your financial goals, risk tolerance, and time horizon.

6. Incremental Approach: Consider taking a gradual approach to investing. Start with a small amount of your extra funds and progressively expand your exposure as you get more comfortable and confident.

7. Long-Term Perspective: If investing a portion of your emergency fund, maintain a long-term approach. Emergency savings, by nature, are created for immediate needs, thus the majority should remain in liquid, low-risk assets.

Your Financial Guardian in Times of Need

In the broad tapestry of personal economics, an emergency fund emerges as a thread that weaves a sense of stability and resilience. It's more than just a monetary reserve; it's your financial guardian, standing ready to shelter you from unexpected storms. Building and maintaining an emergency fund needs perseverance, smart planning, and a commitment to financial well-being.

As you embark on this road, remember that an emergency fund is not a static item but a growing component of your financial environment. It adjusts to your changing circumstances, offering steadiness in times of need.

Basic Living expenditures to consider

Basic living expenses comprise the fundamental costs required to sustain a moderate and pleasant existence. These expenses are crucial for meeting fundamental demands and maintaining a standard of living. While unique situations and geographical regions can impact particular specifics, below is a general outline of fundamental living expenses to consider:

1. Housing:
• Rent or Mortgage: The expense of your residence, whether it's rent for an apartment or mortgage payments for a property.
• Utilities: Expenses including power, water, gas, and rubbish pickup.
• Home Maintenance: Repairs and maintenance costs for your residence.
2. Food:
• Groceries: The expense of purchasing food products for cooking at home.
• Dining Out: Occasional spending for meals at restaurants or take-out.
3. Transportation:
• Car Payments: If you own a car and have financing, enter monthly payments.
• Fuel: The expense of gasoline or other fuels for your car.
• Insurance: Auto insurance for your automobile.
• Public Transportation: Costs for bus, subway, or other public transportation.
• Maintenance: Regular maintenance and sometimes repairs for your vehicle.

4. Healthcare:

• Health Insurance: Premiums for health insurance coverage.

• Prescriptions: The cost of any regular prescriptions.

• Co-pays and Deductibles: Out-of-pocket fees for medical appointments and procedures.

• Dental and Vision Care: Expenses for normal dental and eye care.

5. Utilities:

• Internet and Cable: Monthly rates for Internet and cable television services.

• Phone: Mobile phone or landline expenses.

6. Debt Payments:

• Student Loans: Monthly payments for student loans.

• Credit Card Payments: Minimum payments on credit card balances.

• Other Loans: Payments for personal loans, auto loans, or other obligations.

7. Insurance:

• Life Insurance: Premiums for life insurance coverage.

• Renters or Homeowners Insurance: Insurance coverage for your residence.

• Other Insurance Policies: Any extra insurance policies you may have.

8. Personal Care:

• Toiletries: Expenses for personal care items including soap, shampoo, toothpaste, etc.

• Haircuts and Grooming: Regular grooming expenses.

• Clothes: Budget for necessary clothes purchases.

9. Childcare:

• Daycare or Babysitting: Costs linked with childcare services.

• School Expenses: Uniforms, school supplies, and other relevant costs.

10. Taxes:

• Income Taxes: Account for any income taxes you owe.

• Property Taxes: If you own a home, include property taxes.

11. Savings and Emergency Fund:

• Savings Goals: Contributions towards savings for certain goals.

• Emergency Fund: Regular contributions to an emergency fund for unforeseen needs.

12. Entertainment:

• Streaming Services: Subscription costs for streaming platforms.

• Recreation: Budget for occasional entertainment and leisure activities.

13. Miscellaneous:

• Gifts: Budget for birthdays, holidays, and special occasions.

• Pet Expenses: If you have pets, add food, veterinarian care, and other relevant costs.

• Memberships: Fees for gym memberships, professional associations, or other affiliations.

It's crucial to remember that this list is a basic guide, and particular circumstances may lead to differences. Additionally, discretionary spending such as entertainment and dining out can be changed based on personal preferences and budgetary goals. Creating a thorough budget that matches your individual scenario will help you manage your essential living expenses properly. Regularly monitoring and revising your budget as needed is vital for sustaining financial stability and reaching long-term financial goals.

Chapter 4

Understanding Good and Bad Debt

In the domain of personal finance, the concept of debt often provokes a range of emotions, from worry to empowerment. Debt, ultimately, is a financial instrument – a double-edged sword that, when used carefully, may open the way for advancement and possibilities, but when mishandled, can lead to financial losses and stress.

In this chapter, we'll untangle the distinction between good and bad debt, offering insights into what divides them, how they affect your financial life, and solutions for managing each.

The Basics: What is Debt?

Debt, in its simplest form, is money borrowed with the expectation of repayment, usually with interest, over time. It's a financial agreement where one party lends money to another under agreed-upon terms. Individuals typically incur debt for numerous reasons, such as purchasing big purchases, investing in education, or managing unanticipated bills.

Debt can be broadly classed into two types: good debt and bad debt. The distinction between the two resides in the purpose of the debt and the potential benefits or drawbacks associated with it.

Good Debt: Building for the Future
1. Education Loans:
• Purpose: Loans taken to fund education, such as student loans.
• Rationale: Education is an investment in oneself. Student loans, when managed appropriately, can open doors to better employment options and increased earning potential.
• Benefits: Higher education can lead to enhanced job possibilities, career development, and increased income over the long term.
2. Mortgages:
• Purpose: Loans for acquiring a property.
• Rationale: Buying a home is an important financial objective for many. Mortgages give a road to homeownership without the necessity for upfront, full payment.

• Benefits: Real estate has the potential to appreciate over time, and homeownership can bring security and a sense of accomplishment.

3. Business Loans:

g• Purpose: Loans to establish or expand a business.

• Rationale: Entrepreneurship often requires finance for growth. Business loans can support the formation and expansion of ventures.

• Benefits: Successful businesses create income, contribute to economic progress, and may provide financial security for the business owner.

4. Investment Loans:

• Purpose: Loans for investments, such as margin loans for stock investments.

• Rationale: Investing with borrowed money can enhance prospective rewards.

• Benefits: Successful investments may generate returns that surpass the cost of borrowing, adding to wealth creation.

5. Real Estate Investments:

• Purpose: Loans for real estate investments, such as rental properties.

• Rationale: Real estate can be a successful investment. Loans enable individuals to leverage their investment money.

• Benefits: Rental income, property appreciation, and tax advantages can make real estate investments a source of wealth.

Bad Debt: Cautionary Tales

1. Credit Card Debt:

• Purpose: High-interest debt incurred through credit card usage.

• Rationale: Credit cards offer convenience for everyday expenditures.

• Drawbacks: High interest rates can lead to hefty interest payments, and amassing credit card debt can result in a cycle of financial stress.

2. Auto Loans for Depreciating Assets:

• Purpose: Loans for acquiring autos.

• Rationale: Vehicles are crucial for many, and financing allows for rapid purchase.

• Drawbacks: Vehicles degrade over time, and auto loans may lead to being "upside down," when the outstanding loan total exceeds the vehicle's worth.

3. Payday Loans:

• Purpose: Short-term, high-interest loans primarily meant to cover pressing costs until the next payment.

• Rationale: Access to rapid cash for emergency requirements.

• Drawbacks: Extremely high interest rates can trap individuals in a cycle of debt, making it tough to break free.

4. Consumer Loans for Non-Essential Items:

• Purpose: Loans for non-essential items like luxury products or vacations.

• Rationale: Desire for rapid fulfillment and luxury.

• Drawbacks: Borrowing for non-essential purchases might lead to financial distress and delay progress toward crucial financial goals.

5. Debt for Speculative Investments:

• Purpose: Borrowing to invest in speculative ventures without extensive study.

• Rationale: Expectation of quick and big returns.

• Drawbacks: Speculative investments carry substantial risk, and borrowing to invest in such businesses can result in severe financial losses.

Navigating Debt: Strategies for Success

1. Prioritize High-Interest Debt:

• Action: If you have high-interest debt, such as credit card bills, prioritize paying it down aggressively.

• Rationale: High-interest debt accumulates swiftly and can constitute a severe financial burden. Paying it off immediately saves money on interest payments.

2. Budget Wisely:

• Action: Create a realistic budget that distributes monies for critical spending, debt reduction, and savings.

• Rationale: Budgeting helps you manage your finances properly, ensuring that you allocate resources to key areas and prevent unneeded debt.

3. Emergency Fund:

• Action: Build and maintain an emergency fund to handle unforeseen expenses.

• Rationale: An emergency fund provides a financial safety net, lowering the likelihood of turning to high-interest debt in times of unanticipated hardship.

4. Understand the Terms:
• Action: Before taking on any debt, learn the terms, interest rates, and potential implications.
• Rationale: Informed decisions help you choose debt sensibly and navigate its influence on your financial well-being.

5. Seek Professional Advice:
• Action: Consult with financial professionals for specialized counsel.
• Rationale: Professionals can provide insights customized to your individual situation, helping you make informed decisions regarding controlling and repaying debt.

6. Negotiate Terms:
• Action: If encountering issues with existing debt, consider negotiating with creditors for more favorable terms.
• Rationale: Creditors may be willing to work with you to build a realistic repayment plan, especially if you communicate proactively.

7. Review and Adjust:
• Action: Regularly examine your financial condition and change your debt management strategy as needed.

• Rationale: Life circumstances change, and frequent evaluation ensures that your approach to debt corresponds with your current goals and problems.

A Balanced Approach to Debt

In the broad tapestry of personal economics, debt is a thread sewn into the fabric of many individuals' lives. It can be an instrument for advancement, unlocking opportunities, and facilitating crucial milestones. However, it demands respect and a smart approach.

Understanding the intricacies of good and bad debt helps individuals to make informed financial decisions. It's not about avoiding debt totally but rather negotiating its landscape with understanding and prudence. Good debt, when used correctly, has the potential to be an ally on the path to financial success. Meanwhile, bad debt acts as a cautionary tale, reminding folks to walk carefully and avoid traps that might lead to financial misery.

On the road to financial well-being, striking a balance is crucial. Leveraging good debt to build a brighter future while managing and eliminating bad debt ensures a sustainable and resilient financial landscape.

It's a journey of ongoing learning, adaptation, and empowerment — a journey where debt, when faced with mindfulness, becomes a stepping stone rather than a stumbling obstacle.

Types of debt

Debt comes in several forms, each having different goals and carrying distinct features. Understanding the varieties of debt is vital for making informed financial decisions. Here's an overview of common sorts of debt:

1. Mortgage Debt:

• Purpose: Used to finance the acquisition of real estate, often a home.

• Characteristics: Mortgages are long-term loans with the property serving as collateral. They often have fixed or adjustable interest rates.

2. Auto Loans:

• Purpose: Borrowing to purchase a vehicle, either new or old.

• Characteristics: Auto loans have a specified period, usually ranging from three to seven years, and the vehicle serves as security.

3. Student Loans:

• Purpose: Financing academic expenses, including tuition, books, and living costs.
• Characteristics: Student loans may have fixed or variable interest rates. Repayment frequently begins when the borrower graduates or leaves school.

4. Personal Loans:
• Purpose: Unsecured loans for various personal expenses, such as debt consolidation, medical bills, or home improvements.
• Characteristics: Personal loans are not backed by collateral, and interest rates may be fixed or variable.
5. Credit Card Debt:
• Purpose: Short-term finance for daily purchases.
• Characteristics: Credit cards give a revolving source of credit. If the debt is not paid in full by the due date, interest accrues.
6. Home Equity Loans:
• Purpose: Borrowing against the equity in your house for objectives like home improvements or debt consolidation.
• Characteristics: Home equity loans use your home as collateral and often have set interest rates.
7. Home Equity Lines of Credit (HELOC):

• Purpose: Similar to home equity loans, but with a revolving line of credit.

• Characteristics: HELOCs allow borrowers to draw on the line of credit as needed, with variable interest rates.

8. Payday Loans:

• Purpose: Short-term, small-dollar loans are often repaid on the borrower's next payday.

• Characteristics: Payday loans frequently feature high fees and interest rates, making them an expensive type of borrowing.

9. Business Loans:

• Purpose: Financing for business-related expenses, including startup charges, expansion, or operations needs.

• Characteristics: Business loans vary in terms and form, and they might be secured or unsecured.

10. Peer-to-Peer Loans:

• Purpose: Online platforms connect borrowers with independent lenders for personal or corporate loans.

• Characteristics: Interest rates and periods are defined by the platform, and loans may be unsecured or partially secured.

11. Secured vs. Unsecured Debt:

• Secured Debt: Backed by collateral (e.g., a home or car). If the borrower defaults, the lender can confiscate the collateral.

• Unsecured Debt: Not backed by collateral. Lenders rely on the borrower's creditworthiness, and if the borrower defaults, the lender has limited recourse.

12. Installment Debt vs. Revolving Debt:

• Installment Debt: Loans with defined terms and regular payments until the balance is repaid (e.g., mortgages, auto loans).

• Revolving Debt: Credit lines with flexible repayments based on the outstanding balance (e.g., credit cards, HELOCs).

13. Government Loans:

• Purpose: Loans issued or guaranteed by government institutions for specified objectives, such as home acquisition (FHA loans) or education (Federal Student Loans).

14. Balloon Loans:

• Characteristics: These loans include reduced monthly payments with a high "balloon" payment payable at the end of the term.

15. Convertible Debt:

• Purpose: Often employed in business finance, convertible debt starts as a loan and can convert into equity (ownership) under certain conditions.

16. Tax-Advantaged Debt:

• Purpose: Some types of debt, like mortgage and student loan interest, may offer tax advantages, allowing borrowers to deduct interest payments from their taxable income.

17. Refinanced Debt:

• Purpose: Refinancing entails replacing an existing debt with a new one, sometimes to get better terms or cheaper interest rates.

Understanding the subtleties of each type of debt is vital for efficient financial management. It lets individuals make informed decisions based on their financial goals, risk tolerance, and overall financial well-being.

Tips for Managing Debt

Effectively managing debt is vital for preserving financial stability and working towards long-term financial goals. Here are some practical tips to help you handle your debt wisely:

1. Create a Detailed Budget:

• Action: List all sources of income and itemize your monthly spending.

• Rationale: A budget provides a clear picture of your financial status, helping you arrange funds for debt repayment and important spending.

2. Prioritize High-Interest Debt:

• Action: Identify debts with the highest interest rates and prioritize paying them off first.

• Rationale: Focusing on high-interest debt saves you money in the long term and accelerates the debt repayment process.

3. Negotiate Interest Rates:

• Action: Contact creditors to negotiate reduced interest rates, especially if you have a strong payment history.

• Rationale: Lower interest rates reduce the overall cost of debt, making repayment more reasonable.

4. Consider Debt Consolidation:

• Action: Explore debt consolidation options to merge various loans into a single, more affordable loan.

• Rationale: Consolidation can simplify payments and, if done correctly, may result in a reduced total interest rate.

5. Snowball or Avalanche Method:

• Action: Choose a debt repayment strategy that meets your preferences – the snowball method (paying off the smallest debt first) or the avalanche method (tackling the highest-interest debt first).

• Rationale: Both strategies provide an organized approach to debt repayment, bringing psychological and financial benefits.

6. Build an Emergency Fund:

• Action: Prioritize creating an emergency fund to handle unforeseen expenses without turning to further debt.

• Rationale: An emergency fund works as a financial safety net, avoiding the need to rely on credit cards or loans during unanticipated obstacles.

7. Avoid Accumulating New Debt:

• Action: Resist the urge to accumulate additional debt, especially while working on retiring old loans.

• Rationale: New debt adds to financial stress and can inhibit progress in paying off existing debts.

8. Seek Professional Guidance:

• Action: Consult with financial consultants or credit counselors for specialized help.

• Rationale: Professionals can offer insights on debt management tactics, budgeting, and negotiating with creditors.

9. Understand the Terms of Your Debts:

• Action: Familiarize yourself with the terms, conditions, and fees linked with each obligation.

• Rationale: Understanding the specifics helps you make informed judgments and prevent avoidable charges.

10. Automate Payments:

• Action: Set up automatic payments for at least the minimum amount owing on your bills.

• Rationale: Automation guarantees that payments are made on schedule, preventing late fees and significant damage to your credit score.

11. Review Your Credit Report:

• Action: Regularly review your credit report for accuracy and anomalies.

• Rationale: Monitoring your credit report helps you identify and address any concerns that could damage your credit score.

12. Stay Organized:

• Action: Keep track of due dates, interest rates, and any interaction with creditors.

• Rationale: Organization helps you remain on top of your financial commitments and avoid late payments.

13. Educate Yourself:

• Action: Invest time in studying personal money, debt management tactics, and ways to enhance your financial literacy.

• Rationale: Knowledge helps you to make informed decisions and tackle financial issues more successfully.

14. Celebrate Milestones:

• Action: Acknowledge and celebrate your progress as you pay off bills.

• Rationale: Celebrating milestones promotes motivation and reinforces healthy financial habits.

15. Be Patient and Persistent:

• Action: Recognize that debt repayment is a gradual process that demands consistency.

• Rationale: Patience and persistence are crucial to successfully managing and lowering debt over time.

Remember, effective debt management is not only about paying off what you owe but also about creating healthy financial habits that contribute to long-term financial well-being. By applying these suggestions and keeping

Committed to your financial goals, you may travel the route to debt liberation and financial liberty.

Chapter 5

Budgeting and Financial Well-Being

Budgeting is the cornerstone of solid financial management, providing a roadmap for individuals to invest their income intelligently, fulfill financial goals, and build a secure future. In this comprehensive tutorial, we'll study the principles of budgeting, breaking down complex concepts into simple words to empower everyone, regardless of financial expertise, to take charge of their finances.

What is a Budget?

A budget is a thorough plan that details how you want to manage your money. It's effectively a blueprint for your money, helping you allocate funds to different elements of your life, such as housing, grocery, savings, and entertainment.

Why Budget?

Budgeting has various benefits, including:

1. Financial Control: Knowing where your money is going empowers you to make informed decisions and minimize financial hardship.

2. Goal Achievement: Whether it's saving for a vacation, buying a home, or paying off debt, a budget helps you work towards your financial objectives.

3. Emergency Preparedness: Having a budget helps you to set aside funds for unforeseen needs, creating a financial safety net.

4. Debt Management: By analyzing your expenditures and prioritizing debt payments, you can prevent accruing excessive debt and work towards becoming debt-free.

Key Components of a Budget

1. Revenue: Start by noting all sources of revenue, including your salary, freelance employment, side hustles, and any other monetary inputs.

2. Spending: Categorize your spending into fixed and variable categories. Fixed expenses, such as rent and mortgage payments, stay steady each month, but variable expenses, like groceries and entertainment, may change.

3. Savings and Investments: Allocate a percentage of your income towards savings and investments. Contributions to an emergency fund, retirement accounts, or other savings goals are examples of options that fall within this category.

4. Debt Repayment: If you have outstanding obligations, allocate funds for monthly repayments. Spend less money on interest payments by giving higher-interest debts higher priority.

5. Discretionary Spending: Plan for discretionary spending on non-essential items like dining out, entertainment, and hobbies. This category provides for freedom and fun within your budget.

Creating Your Budget: Step-by-Step Guide

Step 1: Gather Financial Information

Collect information regarding your income, including your salary stubs, freelance revenue, or any other sources of money. Gather statements and bills to understand your typical spending.

Step 2: List Your Sources of Income

Write down all sources of income, including your major work, side gigs, rental income, or any other money you receive regularly.

Step 3: Categorize Your Expenses

Divide your spending into fixed and variable categories. Fixed expenses stay largely consistent, but variable expenses may shift month to month.

Step 4: Identify Essential and Non-Essential Expenses

Distinguish between essential expenses (e.g., housing, utilities, and groceries) and non-essential expenses (e.g., dining out, entertainment, subscriptions).

Step 5: Set Realistic Goals

Your budget should fit with these objectives.

Step 6: Allocate Funds to Categories

Assign exact amounts to each spending category based on your income and priorities. Ensure that your total expenses do not surpass your revenue.

Step 7: Savings and Investments

Allocate a percentage of your salary to savings and investing. This can include an emergency fund, retirement accounts, or other savings goals.

Step 8: Debt Repayment

If you have outstanding obligations, allocate funds for monthly repayments. Prioritize high-interest obligations to minimize interest payments.

Step 9: Discretionary Spending

Allocate funds for discretionary expenditure on non-essential products. This category provides for freedom and fun within your budget.

Step 10: Regularly Review and Adjust

Regularly examine your budget to verify that it corresponds with your financial goals and lifestyle. Adjustments should be made as necessary in response to changes in either income or expenses.

Tips for Successful Budgeting

1. Start Small:

• Action: If you're new to budgeting, start with a simple plan. As you feel more comfortable, you can add more details and categories.

2. Track Your Spending:

• Action: Keep a log of your daily costs to uncover spending patterns.

• Rationale: Tracking expenditure provides significant insights into where your money goes and places where you might cut back.

3. Emergency Fund:

• Action: Prioritize creating an emergency fund to handle unforeseen expenses.

• Rationale: An emergency fund works as a financial safety net, minimizing the need to rely on credit in times of disaster.

4. Be Realistic:

• Action: Set reasonable goals and expectations in your budget.

• Rationale: A budget that matches your actual income and expenses is more likely to be sustainable and productive.

5. Plan for Irregular Expenses:

• Action: Anticipate and budget for irregular expenses, such as annual subscriptions or maintenance charges.

• Rationale: Planning for irregular expenses eliminates financial surprises and ensures that you have funds set aside.

6. Review and Adjust:

• Action: Regularly examine your budget and make modifications as needed.

• Rationale: Life circumstances vary, and your budget should adapt to reflect these changes.

7. Involve Your Family:

• Action: If you share finances with a spouse or family, involve them in the budgeting process.

• Rationale: Joint budgeting encourages transparency and ensures that everyone is on the same page about budgetary goals and priorities.

8. Use Budgeting Tools:

• Action: Explore budgeting apps or solutions to streamline the process.

• Rationale: Technology can ease budgeting, automate tracking, and provide visual representations of your financial picture.

9. Celebrate Milestones:

• Action: Acknowledge and appreciate victories and milestones in your financial journey.

• Rationale: Celebrating accomplishment promotes motivation and fosters favorable financial habits

Common Budgeting Methods

1. Zero-Based Budgeting:
• Concept: Allocate every dollar of your revenue to specified categories, guaranteeing that your income minus expenses equals zero.

2. 50/30/20 Rule:
• Concept: Allocate 50% of your income to needs, 30% to wants, and 20% to savings and debt repayment.

3. Envelope System:
• Concept: Allocate funds to multiple envelopes for certain expenditure categories.
Once an envelope is empty, no further spending in that category until the following budgeting month.

4. Pay Yourself First:
• Concept: Prioritize savings by setting aside a percentage of your income first, before allocating funds to other expenses.

5. Bi-Weekly Budgeting:
• Concept: Plan your budget based on a bi-weekly (every two weeks) income cycle, aligning with many people's pay dates.

6. Percentage-Based Budgeting:

• Concept: Allocate a particular amount of your money to different spending categories based on your priorities.

Mastering Your Financial Future

Budgeting is not a one-size-fits-all exercise; it's a personalized journey that changes with your life and financial goals. By knowing the foundations, executing practical measures, and using budgeting strategies that suit your preferences, you acquire control over your finances. Remember, budgeting is a tool for financial empowerment.

It's not about restriction but about matching your spending with your principles and priorities. Through constant effort, regular review, and a commitment to your financial well-being, you may walk the route to financial success and create a future that matches your objectives.

Spending Less

Spending less also referred to as frugality or cost-consciousness, is a financial technique that entails intentionally minimizing and regulating your costs.

The idea is to live within or below your means, allowing you to save more, pay off debt, and attain financial goals. Spending less does not necessarily imply denying yourself of essentials or indulgences; instead, it's about making informed choices, prioritizing requirements over wants, and finding ways to optimize the value of your money. Here's a detailed tutorial on spending less in simple terms: Understanding Spending Less: Why is it Important?

1. Financial Stability:

• Benefit: Spending less helps you retain financial stability by ensuring that your expenses do not exceed your income.

• Action: Prioritize essential expenses, such as housing, utilities, and groceries, and be wary of discretionary spending.

2. Debt Reduction:

• Benefit: Spending less frees up money that can be used to pay off debts.

• Action: Focus on repaying high-interest loans first and avoid amassing additional debt through wasteful spending.

3. Savings and Investments:

• Benefit: By spending less, you can dedicate more money towards savings and investments.

• Action: Create a budget that contains a set amount for savings, emergency cash, and long-term investments.

4. Financial Freedom:

• Benefit: Spending less adds to financial independence, providing you the ability to make choices based on your preferences rather than financial restraints.

• Action: Evaluate your spending patterns and discover areas where you might reduce back without jeopardizing your well-being.

5. Emergency Preparedness:

• Benefit: Spending less allows you to develop an emergency fund, offering a financial safety net for unexpected needs.

• Action: Set aside a percentage of your salary expressly for emergency funds to cover unanticipated emergencies.

6. Value Maximization:

• Benefit: Spending less fosters attentive consumption, focusing on value and quality rather than quantity.

• Action: Consider the long-term worth of purchases and invest in products that correspond with your needs and deliver enduring satisfaction.

7. Reduced Stress:

• Benefit: Financial stress is often linked to overspending. Spending less minimizes financial burden and increases peace of mind.

• Action: Cultivate a mindset that values financial security and prioritizes needs over transient desires.

Practical Tips for Spending Less

1. Create a Budget:

• Action: Outline your income and expenses, setting boundaries for each category.

• Rationale: A budget provides a clear picture of your financial status, making it easier to discover opportunities for cost-cutting.

2. Differentiate Between Needs and Wants:

• Action: Prioritize requirements like shelter, food, and utilities over discretionary wants.

• Rationale: Distinguishing between needs and wants helps you make more informed spending decisions.

3. Shop Smart:

• Action: Compare costs, look for savings, and consider buying generic or store-brand products.

• Rationale: Smart purchasing helps you to get the same or similar things at a reduced cost.

4. Meal Planning:

• Action: Plan meals, buy goods in bulk, and minimize eating out.

• Rationale: Meal planning decreases food expenses and minimizes the temptation to purchase takeout or dine at restaurants.

5. Use Cash:

• Action: Consider utilizing cash for discretionary expenditures, as it gives a physical boundary.

• Rationale: Using cash makes it more evident when you're reaching your spending limit, helping control impulsive purchases.

6. Automate Savings:

• Action: Set up automatic transfers to your savings account.

• Rationale: Automating savings guarantees that you consistently set aside money, making it a non-negotiable aspect of your budget.

7. Limit Subscription Services:

• Action: Evaluate your subscription services and consider canceling ones you don't usually use.
• Rationale: Subscription charges can build quickly, and removing needless ones helps lower monthly expenses.
8. Buy Used or Secondhand:
• Action: Consider buying used products for specific purchases, such as clothing, furniture, or gadgets.
• Rationale: Secondhand things are sometimes more cheap and can provide excellent value.
9. Negotiate Bills:
• Action: Negotiate with service providers for reduced rates on utilities, internet, and insurance.
• Rationale: Many suppliers are open to bargaining, and achieving cheaper prices can lead to significant savings.

Challenges and Solutions
1. Overcoming Impulse Spending:
• Challenge: Impulse spending might impede efforts to spend less.
• Solution: Implement a waiting time for non-essential purchases to avoid impulsive selections.
2. Social Pressure to Spend:

• Challenge: Social interactions typically include spending, leading to pressure to conform.
• Solution: Communicate your financial goals to friends and family, finding ways to socialize that align with your budget.
3. Unexpected Expenses:
• Challenge: Unforeseen spending can derail budgeting attempts.
• Solution: Build and manage an emergency fund to handle unforeseen needs without turning to extra debt.
4. Lifestyle Adjustments:
• Challenge: Spending less may involve adaptations to lifestyle.
• Solution: Focus on the long-term rewards of financial stability and prioritize what matters to you.
5. Balancing Enjoyment with Frugality:
• Challenge: Balancing fun with frugality can be tough.
• Solution: Find cost-effective methods to enjoy life, such as exploring free or low-cost activities and experiences.

Building a Thriving Financial Future
Spending less is a revolutionary financial habit that helps individuals to take control of their financial futures.

By creating a mindset that values financial well-being, making informed spending decisions, and adopting practical advice, you may achieve a balance between enjoying today and building a secure financial future. Remember, spending less is not about deprivation; it's about conscious choices that fit.

Chapter 6

Multiple Income Sources and Entrepreneurship

Diversifying income sources and engaging in entrepreneurship are techniques that many individuals adopt to achieve financial stability, growth, and independence. Here are some essential factors when researching different revenue streams

Income stream

An income stream refers to the source or sources from which an individual, corporation, or entity earns money or financial gains over a specific period. Income streams can take numerous forms, and they play a significant role in determining the overall financial health and stability of an individual or organization. In this extensive discussion, we will delve into the concept of income streams, analyzing different forms, their value, and the variables impacting their sustainability.

Understanding Income Streams

An income stream is essentially a flow of money into one's possession, often stated in monetary terms, such as salary, dividends, rental income, or earnings from company activity. It reflects the revenue generated from numerous sources, adding to an individual's or entities overall income.

Types of Income Streams

1. Obtained Income: This includes wages, salaries, and bonuses obtained through employment. It is a direct result of human work and time invested in a job.

2. Passive Income: Passive income is created with minimal effort or direct engagement. Rental income, earnings from investments, and royalties from intellectual property are some examples of income and royalty sources.

3. Portfolio Income: This sort of income derives from investments such as stocks, bonds, and mutual funds. Gains or losses from the selling of these assets add to portfolio income.

4. Business revenue: Business owners create revenue through the selling of goods or services. The earnings are obtained after deducting expenses from business income.

Importance of Diversifying Income Streams

• Risk Mitigation: Relying on a single source of income can expose individuals or enterprises to financial dangers. Diversifying revenue streams helps lessen these risks by providing a more robust financial basis.

• Financial Stability: Multiple income streams contribute to financial stability, providing a cushion during economic downturns or unanticipated financial hardships.

• Wealth Accumulation: Diversification allows for the accumulation of wealth through numerous routes. This can lead to a more secure and profitable financial future.

Factors Influencing Income Streams

1. Economic Conditions: Economic issues, such as inflation, interest rates, and overall market circumstances, can affect diverse income sources. For example, rising inflation may reduce the purchasing power of earned money.

2. Market Trends: Income streams connected to investments, such as stocks and real estate, are influenced by market changes. Understanding these tendencies is key to optimizing portfolio income.

3. Technological Advances: Technological advances might generate new economic opportunities or render existing ones obsolete. Adapting to these changes is vital for sustaining income streams in the long run.

4. Government Policies: Tax policy, subsidies, and restrictions can affect the after-tax income from diverse sources. Staying informed about government policy is vital for smart financial planning.

Maximizing and Managing Income Streams

1. Strategic Planning: Developing a thorough financial strategy that incorporates a range of revenue streams is vital. This plan should fit with personal or business goals and consider risk tolerance.

2. Investment Strategies: Effective investment strategies require diversifying across numerous asset classes and businesses. This can include equities, bonds, real estate, and other investment instruments.

3. Skill Development: Enhancing talents and learning new ones might lead to higher earning potential. Continuous learning and adaptation to market demands contribute to the increase of earned revenue.

4. Monitoring and Adjusting: Regularly evaluating income streams and altering strategy based on changing circumstances is crucial. This proactive approach ensures financial resilience and adaptation.

Challenges and Risks Associated with Income Streams

1. Volatility in Markets: Income streams related to investments are sensitive to market volatility. Understanding and controlling these risks is vital for minimizing financial losses.

2. Job Insecurity: Relying primarily on earned income from employment might entail hazards, especially in industries prone to layoffs or economic downturns. Having different revenue streams gives a safety net.

3. Lack of Diversification: Failing to diversify revenue streams might leave individuals or corporations vulnerable to unexpected events. A single-source dependence may lead to financial instability.

4. Legal and Regulatory Risks: Changes in laws and regulations can alter income streams, especially in industries subject to government monitoring. Staying compliant and educated is vital to prevent legal difficulties.

Future Trends and Opportunities in Income Streams
1. Gig Economy: The advent of the gig economy gives chances for individuals to explore numerous revenue streams through freelancing, part-time labor, and short-term projects.
2. Technology and Innovation: Advances in technology create new channels for income generation, such as online enterprises, digital products, and breakthroughs in banking and investing.
3. Remote Work: The shift towards remote employment allows individuals to explore job opportunities abroad, expanding the potential for multiple income sources.
4. Sustainable Investments: Increasing awareness of environmental and social issues is fuelling interest in sustainable investing. Income streams from environmentally friendly and socially responsible ventures are anticipated to grow.

Knowing and efficiently managing revenue streams are key parts of financial well-being. Diversification, strategic planning, and flexibility to shifting economic environments are critical factors in developing and managing a solid financial portfolio. By understanding the numerous sorts of income streams, examining impacting factors, and staying sensitive to developing trends, individuals and enterprises may manage the intricacies of income creation with greater success.

Start Your Business

Starting your own business can be an exciting and gratifying enterprise, but it also needs careful preparation, dedication, and hard labor. Whether you're inspired by a passion, a unique business idea, or a desire for financial independence, the journey of entrepreneurship begins with a solid foundation. Here's a detailed guide to assist you embark on the path of launching your own business:

1. Self-Reflection and Idea Generation:

a. Identify Your Passion and Skills:

• Consider what you are passionate about and where your skills lay.

• Think about areas where you have knowledge or a strong interest.

b. Problem-Solving:

• Look for difficulties or pain points in your own life or your community.

• Your business idea can revolve around giving answers to these difficulties.

c. Market Research:

• Investigate market trends and find gaps or opportunities.

• Analyze your target audience and their needs.

2. Business Planning:

a. Define Your Business Concept:

• Clearly describe what your business will do.

• Define your unique selling proposition (USP) — what sets your firm apart.

b. Conduct a SWOT Analysis:

• Evaluate the Strengths, Weaknesses, Opportunities, and Threats of your business idea.

• Identify how you can capitalize on strengths and mitigate flaws.

c. Create a Business Plan:

• Develop a detailed business plan including your goals, target market, competition, and financial projections.

• A business plan is vital for acquiring capital and managing your business.

3. Legal and Regulatory Considerations:

a. Choose a Business Structure:

• Decide on the legal structure of your business (sole proprietorship, partnership, LLC, corporation).

• Each structure has ramifications for responsibility, taxes, and regulatory obligations.

b. Register Your Business:

• Complete the essential registration and licensing for your business.

• Check local and national rules to verify compliance.

c. Obtain Necessary Permits:

• Some businesses require specific authorization. Research and secure the appropriate licenses.

4. Financial Management:

a. Set Up Financial Systems:

• Open a business bank account and handle separate business money.

• Invest in accounting software or hire an accountant to maintain your financial records.

b. Budgeting and Cash Flow:

• Develop a budget to estimate your startup and operating expenditures.

• Create a cash flow projection to ensure you have sufficient finances to cover expenses.

c. Funding Options:

• Explore financial sources, including personal savings, loans, investors, or crowd funding.

• Consider the financial consequences of each alternative.

5. Building Your Brand:

a. Brand Identity:

• Develop a distinctive brand identity, including a recognizable business name, logo, and tagline.

• Consistency in branding promotes recognition.

b. Establish an Online Presence:

• Construct a website that is both professional and reflective of your business.

• Leverage social media to interact with your audience and market your business.

c. Marketing and Advertising:

• Develop a marketing strategy to promote your products or services.

• Utilize online and offline methods to reach your target demographic.

6. Operational Setup:

a. Location and Equipment:

• Determine whether you need a physical location for your business.

• Acquire the appropriate equipment and technologies.

b. Supply Chain Management:

• Establish relationships with suppliers and vendors.

• Ensure a smooth supply chain for your products or services.

c. Team Building:

• If applicable, hire people who align with your corporate ideals.

• Clearly outline roles and duties within your team.

7. Customer Acquisition and Retention:

a. Customer Relationship Management:

• Focus on building strong relationships with customers.

• Provide exceptional customer service to attract repeat business.

b. Sales Strategies:

• Develop efficient sales techniques to turn leads into customers.

• Consider partnerships or collaborations to extend your reach.

c. Collect Feedback:
• Regularly seek feedback from customers to improve your products or services.
• Adapt your business depending on customer input.
8. Scaling Your Business:
a. Monitor Performance Metrics:
• Track key performance indicators (KPIs) to measure the success of your business.
• Use data to make informed judgments.
b. Explore Growth Opportunities:
• Identify chances for expansion, whether through new products, markets, or partnerships.
• Consider franchising or licensing your business strategy.
c. Stay Adaptive:
• Always be ready to adapt to the ever-changing conditions of the market.
• Stay up to date on the latest developments in technology and trends in the industry.
9. Legal and Ethical Considerations:
a. Compliance:
• Stay current on legal requirements and maintain continuing compliance.

• Protect your firm with appropriate contracts and agreements.

b. Ethics and Social Responsibility:

• Incorporate ethical business practices.

• Consider business social responsibility activities.

10. Personal Development and Well-being:

a. Time Management:

• Effectively manage your time to balance work and personal life.

• Avoid burnout by setting boundaries.

b. Continuous Learning:

• Stay updated about industry developments.

• Invest in your skills and knowledge through continuing study.

c. Networking:

• Build a network of peers, mentors, and advisers.

• Networking can bring significant insights and opportunities.

Establishing your own company is a rewarding and challenging endeavor. It demands a combination of passion, resilience, and strategic thinking. As you manage the complexity of entrepreneurship, realize that each challenge is a chance for progress.

Stay focused on your vision, regularly review your business's performance, and be open to adjusting your methods. With dedication and a well-thought-out plan, you can turn your business idea into a successful venture.

Earn Royalties

Earning royalties can be a lucrative and passive income stream for individuals who create intellectual property, such as writers, musicians, artists, and inventors. Royalties are payments made to the owner of intellectual property for the use or sale of that property. Here are various ways to make royalties:

1. Writing and Publishing:

a. Books:

• Write and publish books. Authors earn royalties on book sales, and these royalties are typically a percentage of the book's retail price.

• Explore traditional publishing or self-publishing options.

b. E-books and Audiobooks:

• Create digital editions of your books to reach a bigger audience.

• Audiobook sales and downloads also provide income for authors.

2. Music:

a. Songwriting:

• Write and compose music. Songwriters get royalties when their songs are performed, recorded, or streamed.

• To receive royalties, register your songs with a performance rights organization (PRO).

b. Recorded Music:

• Musicians and recording artists get royalties from the sales, streaming, and licensing of their recorded music.

• Consider distributing your music through online platforms and streaming services.

3. Art and Design:

a. Visual Art:

• Artists can earn royalties from the sale of prints, merchandise featuring their artwork, and licensing deals.

• Collaborate with companies for product licensing.

b. Design:

• Graphic designers and product designers can earn royalties when their creations are used on items.

• Explore licensing agreements with manufacturers and retailers.

4. Inventions and Patents:

a. Product Inventions:

• Inventors can earn royalties by licensing their inventions to firms for manufacturing and distribution.

• Obtain a patent to protect your idea and negotiate licensing terms.

b. Technology Patents:

• Tech innovators can earn royalties through licensing agreements for their patented technology.

• Consider engaging with patent licensing services or negotiating directly with firms.

5. Photography:

a. Stock Photography:

• Photographers can earn royalties by selling their photos through stock photography websites.

• Create high-quality and original photographs that have market demand.

b. Prints and Merchandise:

• Sell prints of your photographs and license your images for use in ads, periodicals, and goods.

6. Film and Television:

a. Screenwriting:

• Write scripts for films or television shows. Screenwriters might receive royalties from the sale or production of their work.

• Register scripts with appropriate industry associations.

b. Participation Agreements:

• Negotiate participation agreements that pay a share of income for performers, directors, and producers based on the success of a film or TV show.

7. Software and Apps:

a. Software Development:

• Developers can earn royalties from the sales or subscriptions of their software applications.

• Explore app markets, software platforms, or license agreements.

b. Mobile Apps:

• App creators can make royalties through in-app purchases, adverts, and premium features.

• Consider offering a free version with optional premium upgrades.

8. Real Estate:

a. Mineral Rights:

• If you own land with mineral rights, you can earn royalties from corporations that extract and sell minerals.

• Negotiate leasing agreements with mining or drilling businesses.

9. Franchising:

a. Franchise Ownership:

• If your business strategy is profitable, think about franchising it. Franchise owners collect royalties from franchisees based on their revenue.

• Provide extensive assistance and guidance to franchisees.

10. Online Content:

a. YouTube and Streaming:

• Content creators on platforms like YouTube earn ad money and, in some situations, gain royalties from the usage of their content on other sites.

• Join YouTube's Partner Program or investigate streaming providers.

b. Online Courses & E-Learning:

• Create and sell online courses. Earn royalties from course sales or subscriptions.

• Utilize platforms specialized in online schooling.

11. Licensing Agreements:

a. Brand Licensing:

• License your brand name or logo for use on items. Earn royalties from licensed merchandise.

• Ensure that licensing agreements safeguard your brand identity.

b. Character Licensing:

• If you've created memorable characters, try licensing them for use in goods, animations, or other media.

• Negotiate terms that match with the character's popularity.

Earning royalties involves not just creative talent but also smart administration of your intellectual property. It's vital to protect your work through copyrights, patents, or other legal measures. Additionally, understanding the terms of licensing agreements and remaining involved with industry developments will contribute to the long-term viability of your royalty-based income streams.

Invest in Rental Properties

Investing in rental properties may be a rewarding enterprise, providing a consistent income stream and the potential for long-term gain. However, like any investment, it comes with hazards and requires careful planning. Here's a thorough guide to help you manage the process of investing in rental properties:

1. Define Your Investment Goals:

a. Cash Flow vs. Appreciation:

• Determine whether you're primarily seeking rental revenue (positive cash flow) or long-term property appreciation.

• Your investment plan may differ depending on your goals.

b. Short-Term vs. Long-Term:

• Decide if you're seeking short-term gains through property flipping or long-term wealth creation through rental income.

2. Research and Market Analysis:

a. Location:

• Research possible locations for rental properties. Consider aspects such as job growth, demographic trends, and amenities.

• Look for neighborhoods with a high demand for rentals.

b. Property Types:

• Explore numerous types of rental properties, including single-family homes, multi-family units, or commercial properties.

• To choose the best kind of property, evaluate the local real estate market.

Market Trends:
• Stay informed about local and national real estate market developments.
• Understand the possibility of property value appreciation in your chosen market.
3. Financial Planning:
a. Budgeting:
• Set a realistic budget that includes the purchase price, closing charges, renovation expenses, and ongoing operational costs.
• Factor in prospective vacancies and upkeep expenditures.
b. Financing Options:
• Explore finance choices, including mortgages and loans.
• Assess your creditworthiness and request pre-approval for a mortgage.
c. Return on Investment (ROI):
• Calculate the probable return on investment by factoring rental revenue, expenses, and property appreciation.
• Aim for a positive cash flow.
4. Due Diligence:
a. Property Inspection:

• Conduct a comprehensive assessment of the property to discover any structural issues or needed repairs.

• Factor in refurbishment expenditures while calculating the overall investment.

b. Legal Considerations:

• Review local zoning rules, building codes, and landlord-tenant restrictions.

• Ensure compliance with legal regulations for renting out a home.

5. Property Management:

a. Self-Management vs. Hiring a Manager:

• Decide if you'll manage the property yourself or engage a professional property management company.

• Property managers perform activities like tenant screening, rent collecting, and maintenance.

b. Tenant Screening:

• Implement a thorough tenant screening process to limit the possibility of late payments or property damage.

• Check rental history, credit scores, and references.

c. Lease Agreements:

• Draft thorough lease agreements that outline tenant responsibilities, rental terms, and eviction policies.

• Consult legal professionals to guarantee lease compliance with local legislation.

6. Maintenance and Upkeep:

a. Regular Inspections:

• Conduct frequent property inspections to identify and address maintenance issues promptly.

• Proactive maintenance can prevent costly problems in the long run.

b. Emergency Fund:

• Establish an emergency fund to cover unanticipated repairs or periods of vacancy.

• Having financial reserves allows you may solve difficulties without jeopardizing your cash flow.

7. Networking and Education:

a. Real Estate Networks:

• Join local real estate investment clubs and networks to interact with experienced investors and experts.

• Learn from the experiences of others in the real estate sector.

b. Continuous Learning:

• Stay informed on real estate trends, market changes, and investment methods.

• Attend workshops, and seminars, and read relevant material to increase your understanding.

8. Exit Strategies:

a. Sell or Hold:

• Determine your departure strategy. Are you looking to sell the property for a profit, or do you want to hold it for long-term rental income?

• Be adaptable and change your plan depending on market conditions.

b. Tax Implications:

• Understand the tax ramifications of selling or holding a rental property.

• Consult with tax professionals to improve your tax plan.

9. Risk Management:

a. Insurance:

• Obtain enough insurance coverage for your rental property.

• Consider liability insurance to guard against unanticipated situations.

b. Market Downturns:

• Acknowledge the cyclical nature of the real estate market.

• Plan for market downturns and have mechanisms in place to weather economic headwinds.

10. Continuous Monitoring and Evaluation:

a. Performance Metrics:

• Regularly monitor the financial performance of your rental property.

• Evaluate whether the property is achieving your investing goals.

b. Adaptability:

• Be adaptable to changing market conditions and adjust your strategies accordingly.

• Stay proactive in managing your investment for long-term success.

Investing in rental properties can be a rewarding endeavor when approached with careful planning and a thorough understanding of the market. By considering factors such as location, financial planning, property management, and risk mitigation, you can build a successful and resilient real estate investment portfolio. Remember that real estate is a long-term investment, and patience, diligence, and ongoing education are key to achieving sustained success in this field.

Get a Side Hustle

Starting a side hustle can be a great way to explore your passions, increase your income, and potentially transition into a full-time entrepreneurial venture. Here's a guide to help you get started with a side hustle:

1. Identify Your Skills and Interests:

a. Passions and Hobbies:

• Consider activities or hobbies you are passionate about.

• Your side hustle is more likely to be sustainable if it aligns with your interests.

b. Skills:

• Identify your skills and expertise. What are you good at?

• Your existing skills can be the foundation for a successful side hustle.

2. Explore Side Hustle Ideas:

a. Freelancing:

• Offer your skills as a freelancer. This could include writing, graphic design, programming, social media management, etc.

• Freelancers and clients are connected by platforms such as Upwork, Fiverr, and Freelancer.

b. Online Selling:

• Sell handmade crafts, vintage items, or even digital products online.
• Platforms like Etsy, eBay, and Amazon provide opportunities for online selling.
c. Consulting:
• Offer consulting services based on your expertise.
• Consulting can be done in various fields such as business, marketing, or career guidance.
d. Tutoring or Coaching:
• Share your knowledge by tutoring or coaching others.
• Students and tutors are connected through platforms like Wyzant and Chegg Tutors.
e. Affiliate Marketing:
• Promote goods and get paid a commission for each purchase made using your own affiliate link.
• Many companies offer affiliate programs, including Amazon Associates and ClickBank.
f. Photography or Videography:
• If you enjoy photography or videography, offer your services for events or stock footage.
• Platforms like Shutterstock or Adobe Stock allow you to sell stock photos and videos.
g. Blogging or Content Creation:

• Create a YouTube channel or blog centered on your hobbies.

• Make money with affiliate marketing, sponsorships, and advertisements.

3. Evaluate Market Demand:

a. Research Your Niche:

• To find out whether there is a market for your side business, do some research.

• Identify competitors and find ways to differentiate your offerings.

b. Validate Your Idea:

• Test the waters by offering your services or products on a small scale.

• Gather feedback and adjust based on customer responses.

4. Set Realistic Goals:

a. Define Objectives:

• Be specific about the goals you have for your side project.

• Whether it's extra income, skill development, or a potential business transition, having clear goals is essential.

b. Time Commitment:

• Regarding the amount of time you may commit to your side project, be reasonable.

• Balancing your main job, personal life, and side hustle requires effective time management.

5. Create a Brand and Online Presence:

a. Branding:

• Create a unique brand identity for your side hustle.

• This includes a memorable name, logo, and consistent visual elements.

b. Online Presence:

• Establish a professional online presence through a website or social media.

• Use platforms like Instagram, LinkedIn, or Twitter to connect with your target audience.

6. Financial Considerations:

a. Budgeting:

• Create a budget for your side hustle, including initial expenses and ongoing costs.

• To guarantee profitability, keep a constant eye on your finances.

b. Pricing Strategy:

• Determine the appropriate pricing for your products or services.

• Consider factors such as market rates, your expertise, and perceived value.

7. Legal and Regulatory Compliance:

a. Business Structure:

• Decide on the legal structure of your side hustle (sole proprietorship, LLC, etc.).

• Speak with an attorney to make sure that local laws are followed.

b. Tax Considerations:

• Recognize the tax ramifications of your side gig earnings.

• Keep detailed records of income and expenses for tax purposes.

8. Network and Collaborate:

a. Networking:

• Connect with others in your industry or niche.

• Attend events, join online communities, and build a network that can offer support and collaboration opportunities.

b. Collaborations:

• Explore collaborations with other individuals or businesses.

• Collaborations can expand your reach and bring new opportunities.

9. Continuous Learning:

a. Skill Development:

• Keep informed on market developments and keep improving your abilities.

• Invest time in learning and adapting to changes in your field.

b. Feedback and Improvement:

• Seek feedback from clients or customers.

• Utilize client input to enhance your products and services.

10. Evaluate and Pivot:

a. Performance Metrics:

• Track key performance indicators (KPIs) relevant to your side hustle.

• Assess your progress on a regular basis and make any strategy adjustments.

b. Adaptability:

• Be open to pivoting your side hustle based on market changes or personal preferences.

• Flexibility is key to long-term success.

Starting a side hustle requires dedication, creativity, and resilience. By carefully planning, staying adaptable, and continuously learning, you can turn your passion or expertise into a successful venture that complements your main source of income. Remember that the journey of entrepreneurship is a learning experience, and each step contributes to your growth and success.

Conclusion

In conclusion, "Financial Knowledge for Young Adults Made Easy" is not simply a learning tool; it's a vital guide influencing the financial environment for the next generation. The complexities of personal finance can be overwhelming, but our simple approach attempts to empower young adults with the knowledge and skills necessary to handle the intricacies of money management. Financial literacy is not a one-time lecture; it's a continuing journey. The simple structure offered here serves as a solid basis, encompassing essential topics from budgeting and saving to investment and debt management. Breaking down these concepts into digestible chunks gives young adults the practical know-how needed to make informed decisions about their finances.

Furthermore, the emphasis on real-world applications guarantees that the theoretical information isn't merely retained in textbooks but becomes a dynamic instrument in the hands of young adults. From building a budget that corresponds with personal goals to comprehending the

Importance of credit ratings, the simplified approach demystifies financial concepts and encourages a feeling of financial responsibility.

This course also highlights the need to cultivate a healthy relationship with money. It encourages young person's not merely to gain wealth but to use their resources intelligently, with a focus on both short-term aims and long-term financial well-being. The incorporation of case studies, relatable examples, and interactive activities brings financial literacy to life, making it a relatable and interesting experience.

As young adults embark on their financial adventures, equipped with the insights learned from this simplified handbook, they are better prepared to face the inevitable problems and seize opportunities that come their way. From the earliest steps of constructing an emergency fund to the intricacies of investing portfolios, this guide presents a path that changes with the financial landscape, assuring relevance in an ever-changing world.

In summary, "Financial Knowledge for Young Adults Made Easy" is not only about numbers and formulas; it's about empowerment and liberty. It educates the next generation with the tools they need to make healthy financial decisions, developing a sense of confidence and control over their financial destinies. As these young adults use these concepts in their lives, they not only safeguard their financial future but contribute to a society that is economically knowledgeable and robust. This guide is not only an education; it's an investment in the future financial well-being of individuals and the greater community.

www.ingramcontent.com/pod-product-compliance
Lightning Source LLC
Chambersburg PA
CBHW071207290526
45796CB00008B/173